July 1995

To our special Little Leah who is now 2 years old. May this book be the beginning of your thirst to know Jesus and a desire to walk faithfully with him. Our prayers will always be with you No matter where you are or what you are doing.

Love always,

Grandpa & Grandma
Farmwald

This book belongs to

_____

Presented by

_____

on

_____

THE TINY TOTS BIBLE STORY BOOK

John and Kim Walton

Illustrated by Alice Craig

Chariot Books™
David C. Cook Publishing Co.

Chariot Books™ is an imprint of David C. Cook Publishing Co.
David C. Cook Publishing Co., Elgin, Illinois 60120
David C. Cook Publishing Co., Weston, Ontario
Nova Distribution Ltd., Newton Abbot, England

TINY TOTS BIBLE STORY BOOK

Cover design: Koechel-Peterson & Associates Inc., Minneapolis, MN

First Printing, 1993
Printed in the United States of America
97 96 95 94 93   5 4 3

Library of Congress Cataloging-in-Publication Data

Walton, John H., 1952-
    Tiny tots Bible story book / John and Kim Walton ; illustrated by Alice Craig.
        p.   cm.
    Summary: Presents fourteen stories from both the Old and New Testaments, retold for preschool children and accompanied by Scripture verses and several simple discussion questions.
        ISBN 0-7814-0834-2
    1.   Bible stories. English. [1. Bible stories.] I. Walton, Kim. II. Craig, Alice, ill. III. Title.
BS551.2.W236 1993
220.9'505—dc20

93-19999
CIP
AC

Portions of this book were previously published:
© 1986 *God and the World He Made; Abraham and His Big Family; Moses and the Mighty Plagues;* and, *Jonah and the Big Fish;*
© 1987 *Adam and Eve in the Garden; Samuel and the Voice in the Night; David Fights Goliath; Jeroboam and the Golden Calves; Elijah and the Contest; Daniel and the Lions; Jesus, God's Son Is Born;* and, *Paul and the Bright Light.*

Table of Contents

God
and the World He Made

9

God made
everything
there is.

11

God made the dry land

and the oceans.

God made the plants
and the trees to grow
in the earth.

**God made the sun,
the moon, and all the
stars to give light to the earth.**

17

God made birds
to fly through the air

and fish to swim in the water.

God made animals

21

animals
of all
kinds!

And then . . .

23

God made people.

Of all the things God made,
people were the most like God.
He made everything for them.

The names of the first people

were Adam and Eve.

God put them in a big,
beautiful garden
and asked them
to take care of it.

Then God was finished making everything,

so he stopped.

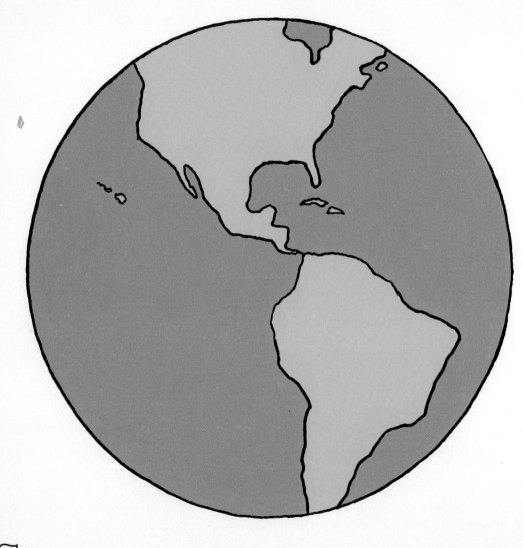

**God saw that
everything
he had made was
just right.**

God made you, too. And

you are special to God.

37

God saw all that he had made, and it was very good.

Genesis 1:31, NIV

1. What did God make?

2. Who is special to God?

Adam and Eve
in the Garden

Adam and Eve were the first people God made.

He put them in a big
garden to live.

God had planted many fruit
trees in the garden.

45

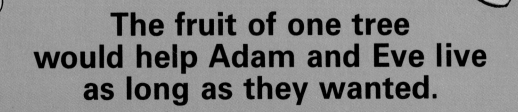

**The fruit of one tree
would help Adam and Eve live
as long as they wanted.**

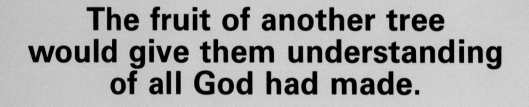

**The fruit of another tree
would give them understanding
of all God had made.**

**Even though Adam and Eve
did not understand many things,
God told them not to eat
from this tree.**

51

God said that if they
disobeyed and ate from that tree,
they would have to die.

53

But a serpent told them that if they ate from that tree, they would understand everything.

They would be like God!

**Adam and Eve listened
to the serpent instead of to God.
They ate the fruit.**

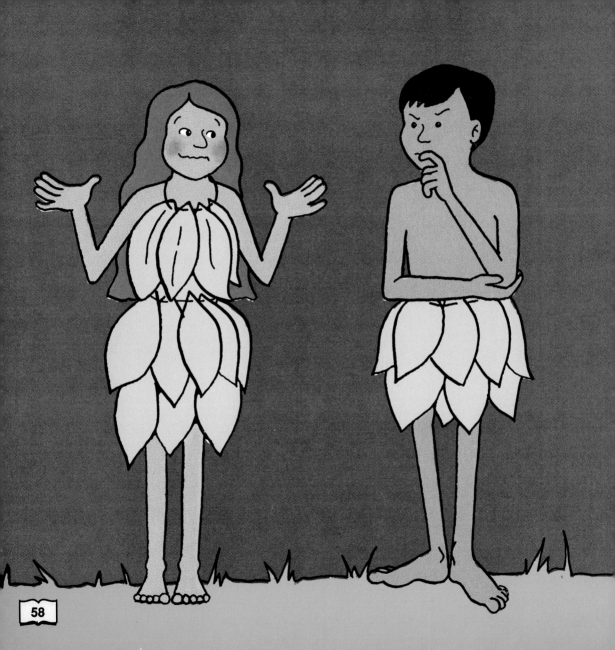

Now they understood about many more things.

Adam and Eve
knew they were wrong
to disobey.

61

God was sad and said they
had to leave the garden.

63

64

They could no longer
eat from the tree that helped them
to live as long as they wanted,
so they grew old and died.

It is best to obey God and follow His plans.

I will obey God's word.

From Psalm 119:17, NIV

1. Who were the first people that God made?

2. What did Adam and Eve do that displeased God?

Noah
and the Flood

Long, long ago, people on the earth were very bad. They were so bad that God was sad He had made them.

The only good person was Noah.

73

God planned to send a big flood to punish the people of the earth.

But first, He told Noah to build a big boat—an ark—so Noah and his family and some animals would be safe.

So Noah built the ark and

put two of
each kind of
animal into it.

79

Then it rained...
for forty days and nights!

After everything on earth was under water, the rain stopped.

83

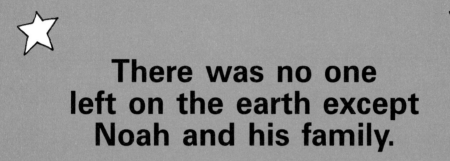

There was no one
left on the earth except
Noah and his family.

85

When the water began
to go down, the ark stopped
on top of a mountain.

After a while, Noah used birds
to find out if he could
leave the ark.

Finally the water dried up enough so everyone could come out of the ark.

Noah and his family thanked God that they were alive.

93

94

God showed them a rainbow to say that He would never destroy the earth by a flood again.

Nothing makes God sadder than when He has to punish the people He made and loves.

Noah did all that the Lord told him to do.

From Genesis 7:5, NIV

1. What did God tell Noah to build?

2. How many days and nights did it rain?

3. What did Noah and his family do after they came out of the ark?

Abraham
and His Big Family

Abraham lived with his family in the city of Ur.

101

One day, God asked Abraham
to do something hard.

God asked him to leave
his country, his family, and
his share of the family's things.

God told Abraham he would give him his own country and a big family—so big that counting his family would be like trying to count the stars!

107

God said that someday, because of Abraham's family, the whole world would be better off.

**Abraham believed
God and left his country
with his wife, Sarah.**

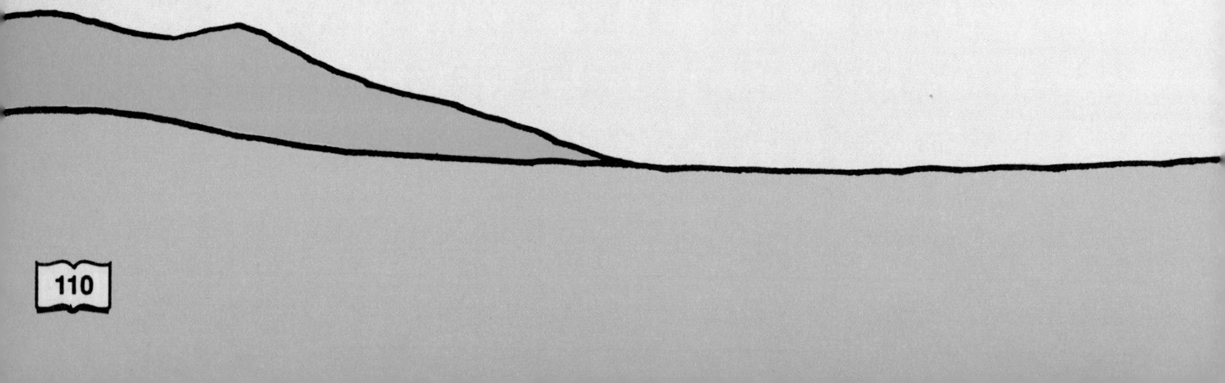

111

God took Abraham
and Sarah to a land that
would one day belong
to their family.

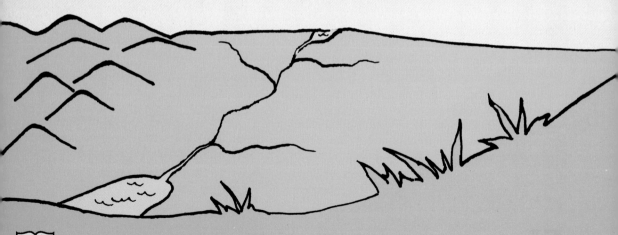

But Abraham and Sarah grew older, and they still had no children.

Finally, when they were
very, very old, they had a son.
They named him Isaac.

Over many years, God gave Abraham a big family, just as he had promised. They were called the Israelites.

119

God gave the Israelites a new land,
Canaan, to be their home—
just as he had promised.

Many, many years later, a special child was born to the family that came from Abraham. It was Jesus!

Just as God had promised, the whole world is better off. Because of Abraham's family, we have the way to know God.

It makes sense to believe
what God says. God always
keeps his promises.

The Lord is faithful to all his promises.

Psalm 145:13, NIV

1. What did God tell Abraham?

2. What does God always do?

Moses
and the Mighty Plagues

The people of Israel were slaves in the land of Egypt.

131

God told Moses to lead
the Israelites out of Egypt
to the land he had
promised to them.

133

But Pharaoh, the king of Egypt, wouldn't let the Israelites go.

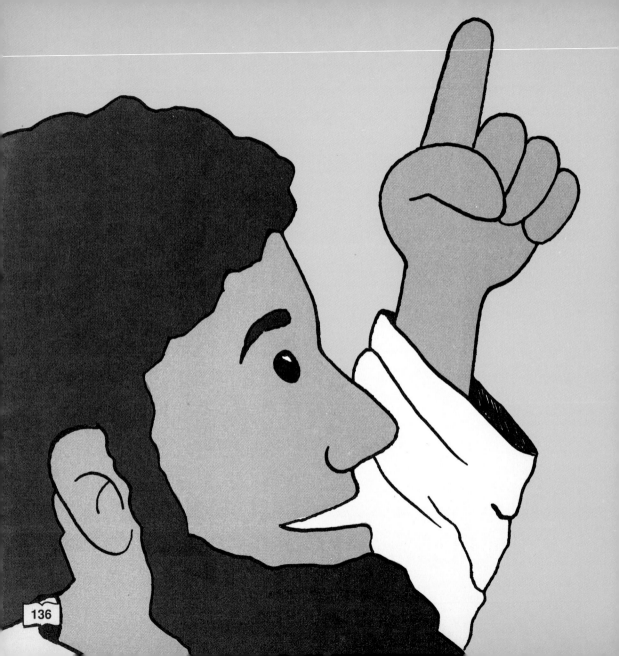

Moses told Pharaoh that God would send plagues on Egypt if Pharaoh didn't let the Israelites leave.

Then there were frogs, then gnats,

and then flies everywhere. 141

But Pharaoh still wouldn't let the people go.

Cattle died,

and Egyptians got sick.

And Pharaoh *still* wouldn't let the Israelites go.

**Then came the last plague:
God told Pharaoh
that the firstborn in every family
would die.**

When the last plague came, Pharaoh finally let the Israelites go.

God had delivered his people, just as he promised.

154

**God is so strong
that nothing can stop him
from keeping his promises.**

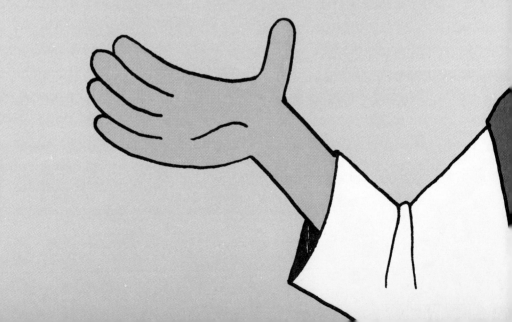

All of God's promises come true.

From Joshua 23:14, NIV

1. What did God tell Moses to do?

2. What are some of the plagues that God sent to the Egyptians?

3. What does God always keep?

Samuel
and the Voice in the Night

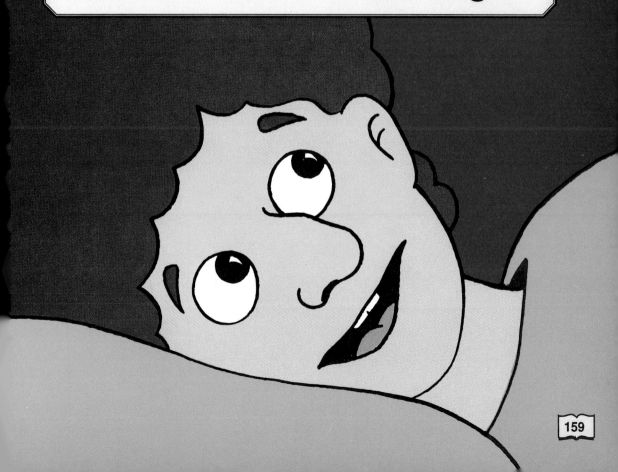

**Samuel lived in the temple
in a city in Israel.**

**Samuel had lived there since
he was a little boy. He was a helper
for Eli, the priest.**

One night, as Samuel slept
in the temple, he heard someone
call his name. He thought
it must be Eli.

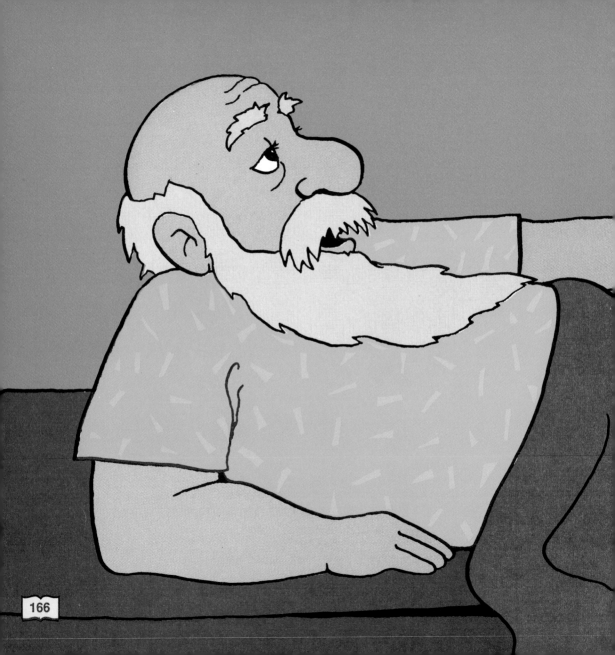

But when Samuel went to Eli, the priest told him to go back to bed.

167

Then Samuel
heard his name
called again.

169

But again, Eli said he had not called.

When Samuel came a third time, Eli knew that the Lord was the one calling Samuel.

Eli told Samuel how to answer the Lord.

175

This time, when Samuel
heard his name, he said, "Speak, Lord.
I'm listening."

The Lord said he was going
to punish Eli's family because they
did not honor the Lord. They had
disobeyed God's law.

In the morning, Samuel had
to tell Eli what the Lord had said.

183

**God often spoke to Samuel
after that night. Everyone knew he was
God's chosen leader for Israel.**

God has special jobs for those
who listen and obey.

Listen to God.

From Deuteronomy 30:20, NIV

1. Who called Samuel's name at night?

2. What did Samuel tell the Lord?

3. Who does God choose for special jobs?

David
Fights Goliath

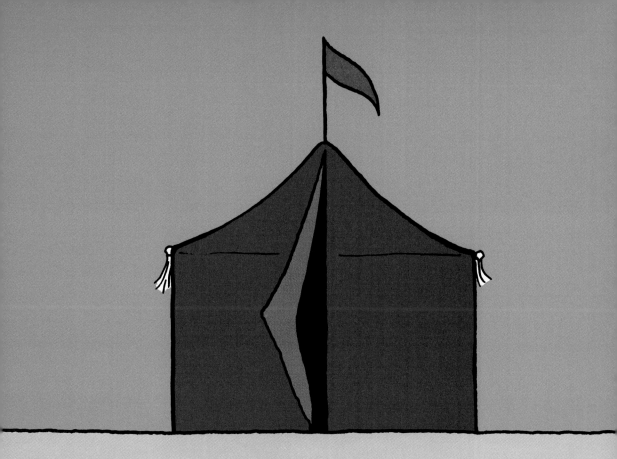

King Saul and the people of Israel were at war with the Philistines.

David was not fighting in the war. He stayed at home to take care of the sheep.

193

Sometimes David's father
sent him to the army camp to see how
his soldier brothers were doing.

David always wanted to hear about the war.

197

On one of David's visits, he heard about a Philistine warrior named Goliath, who was big and strong.

Goliath wanted the Israelites to send someone to fight against him, but they were all afraid.

David believed the Lord
would help him, so he offered
to fight Goliath.

King Saul warned David that Goliath had been a soldier for a long time and was very good at fighting.

But David was sure the Lord
would help him win.

When Saul offered David his armor, David said no because he wasn't used to fighting with armor on.

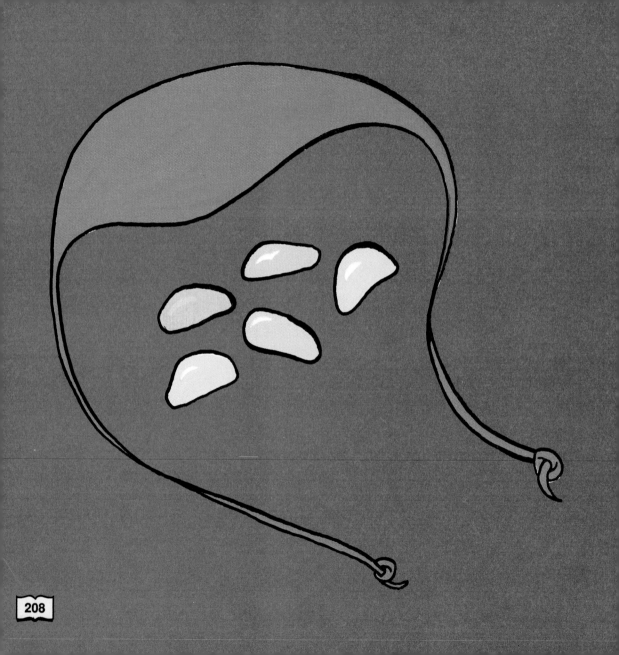

**David took his sling
and went out to fight Goliath.**

When Goliath saw him coming, he made fun of David.

But David used his stone and sling,
and the Lord helped him win the fight.

**David was right to believe
that the Lord was the strongest of all.**

Great is our Lord.
Psalm 147:5, NIV

1. What did David use to fight Goliath?

2. Who helped David fight the giant?

3. Who was stronger—Goliath or the Lord?

Jeroboam
and the Golden Calves

220

Jeroboam was one of King Solomon's highest officials in the land of Israel.

221

One day a prophet named Ahijah
came to visit
Jeroboam.

Ahijah tore a coat into twelve
pieces, one for each of the tribes
of Israel. He gave ten pieces
to Jeroboam.

Ahijah said the Lord was going to make
Jeroboam king of ten of the tribes
after King Solomon died.

When King Solomon heard about this,
he was angry. He wanted *his* son to be king
after him. Jeroboam had to leave the
country quickly.

But after Solomon died,
Jeroboam did become king of the
ten tribes. Only two tribes were left for
Solomon's son, Rehoboam.

Jeroboam did not want his tribes to go to the Temple in Jerusalem, where Solomon's son, Rehoboam, was the king.

So he set up golden calves in two temples where his people worshiped. The calves were supposed to be thrones for the Lord.

Jeroboam thought he was doing a good thing, but this is the wrong way to worship the Lord.

The people began to think
that the calves themselves were gods.

Then the prophet Ahijah came back . . . and was he upset! Ahijah told Jeroboam that the Lord was very angry about the calves.

241

But Jeroboam never took the calves
down. Neither did any of the kings
of Israel who ruled after his death.

God finally had to punish the people of Israel, because they did not treat Him as the one true God.

It is very important to worship God in the right way. It is always a big mistake to think we can force God to do what we want Him to do.

Worship the Lord your God.

Deuteronomy 6:13, NIV

1.   What did the prophet give
     Jeroboam?

2.   What did Jeroboam make for
     the people to worship?

Elijah
and the Contest

Elijah was a prophet of the Lord in Israel. God gave messages through him.

The king and queen
of Israel were named
Ahab and Jezebel.

Ahab and Jezebel wanted
all Israel to worship
a false god, Baal,
as well as the Lord.

**Baal was supposed to be
the god of rain and
lightning.
He was supposed
to help food grow.**

But the Lord said
people should worship
only him, not Baal.
Elijah told King Ahab
that the Lord would
hold back the rain
so no food
would grow.

The Lord stopped any rain from falling for a long time to show the people that Baal wasn't really a god.

261

After a while, Elijah
challenged the prophets
of Baal to a contest
on Mt. Carmel.

The prophets of Baal
put a sacrifice on
the altar to Baal.
They prayed for
Baal to send fire.

They prayed all day,
but no fire came.

**Then Elijah put a sacrifice
on the altar to the Lord.**

Elijah poured water all over it.

271

When Elijah prayed,
the Lord sent fire right away.

Then the Lord said
he would send rain.
And he did.

There is no God but the Lord
—not in Elijah's day
and not today.

The Lord—he is God!

I Kings 18:39, NIV

1. What was the name of the prophet of God?

2. Who did the king and queen want the people to worship?

Daniel
and the Lions

Daniel was one of
the three leaders of
the Persian Empire.

Darius, the king, liked
Daniel best, so the other
leaders were jealous.

They always tried to catch
Daniel doing something wrong.

But they couldn't, because Daniel always tried to do what God wanted him to.

285

Three times each day, Daniel prayed
to the one true God. The other leaders
decided to use this to get
Daniel in trouble.

They got King Darius
to give a command
they could use to get
Daniel in trouble.

**Anyone who disobeyed
this command would
be thrown into a
cave of hungry lions.**

The next day, when Daniel went to pray, the other leaders caught him and took him to Darius.

292

293

They said that Daniel had disobeyed
the king's command and would have
to be thrown to the lions.

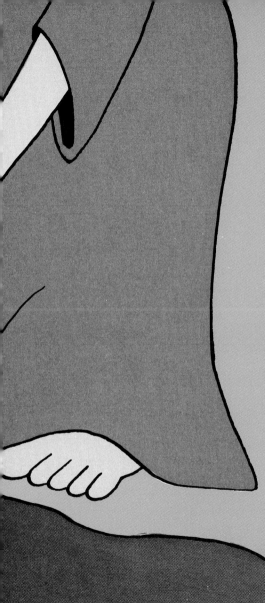

But there was no
way that Darius
could help Daniel.
So Daniel was
thrown into
the cave of
hungry lions.

But God protected Daniel, and
the lions did not hurt him.

Darius was glad that Daniel was safe.
He punished the men who had
tried to hurt Daniel.

Darius gave a command that everyone should praise Daniel's God.

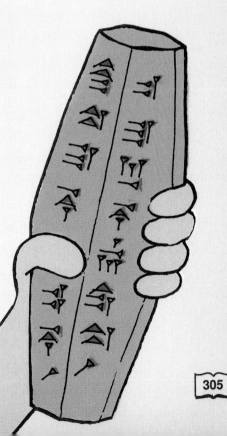

God protected Daniel because Daniel always tried to do what God wanted him to.

307

God rescued Daniel from the lions.

From Daniel 6:27, NIV

1. How many times each day did Daniel pray to God?

2. What did some men do to Daniel because he prayed to God?

3. What did God do to help Daniel?

Jonah
and the Big Fish

**God told Jonah to go
and speak to the people
of Nineveh.**

Jonah did not want to
speak to Nineveh, so he ran.
He got on a boat going far away.

But God sent a big storm, and everyone was afraid.

Jonah told the sailors to throw him into the sea, and God would stop the storm.

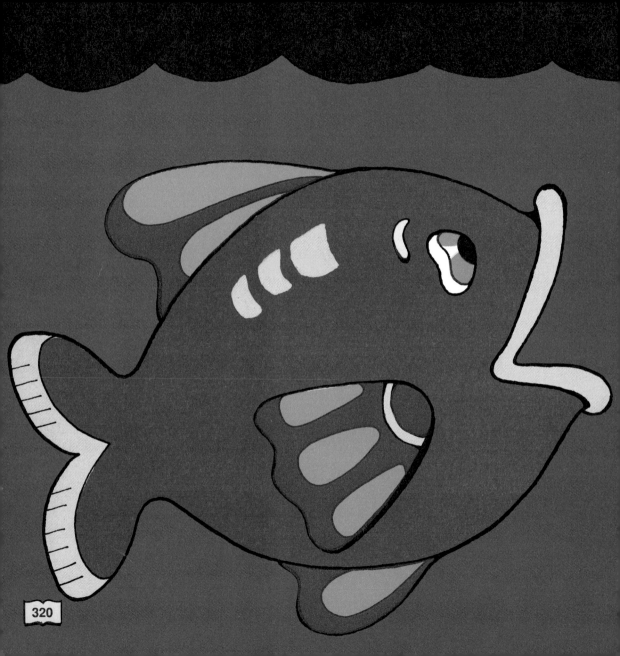

**But God sent
a big fish to save him.**

Jonah was glad to be alive, but he still did not want to go to Nineveh.

**Again God told Jonah to
go speak to the people of Nineveh.
This time Jonah went,
even though he did not want to.**

Jonah said, "In forty days your city will be destroyed."

The people thought,
"If we are good, maybe
God will not destroy our city."

Thank You!

Jonah was angry.
He didn't think Nineveh
should get another chance
just for being good.

**But God showed Jonah
that he should not be angry,
because sometimes
he needed God's help, too.**

**God likes to help us
by giving us second chances
when we want to obey him.**

Obey the Lord your God.

Jeremiah 26:13, NIV

1. What did God tell Jonah to do?

2. What happened to Jonah because he did not obey God?

Jesus,
God's Son Is Born

339

Mary and Joseph were about to have a baby.

An angel told
them their baby
would be the
Son of God.

341

Just before the baby came,
Mary and Joseph had to
take a trip to Bethlehem.

When they got to Bethlehem, they couldn't find any place to stay.

Finally they found a stable—and that's where the baby was born!

347

**Angels spread
the news of this special
baby—God's Son.**

Shepherds heard about it from the angels and ran to see the baby Jesus.

They
worshipped
Him.

355

Even the stars
spread the news in
their own way.

**Wise Men far away saw
a special star.**

**They knew that a
King had been born—Jesus!**

The Wise Men brought gifts to honor Him.

God born as a
baby boy! This was the most
important thing that had
ever happened . . .

because Jesus is the most important part of God's plan for the world.

The Savior is born in Bethlehem.

From Luke 2:11, NIV

1. Where was baby Jesus born?

2. Who came to see the new baby?

3. Who brought gifts for baby Jesus?

Jesus
and the Empty Tomb

Many people heard Jesus teach,
but some of them didn't like Jesus.
They didn't believe He was
God's Son.

Those who
didn't like Jesus
came to take
Him away one
night while He
prayed.

373

When they got Jesus back
to Jerusalem, they made
fun of Him and hurt Him.

Then they took Him out to
a hill to hang on a cross
and die.

It's sad to think of
God's Son nailed
to a cross;

but Jesus was willing to die because He loved us.

382

Jesus' friends put His body into a cave called a tomb. Then they covered the opening with a big rock.

**Soldiers came to guard
the tomb.**

On Sunday morning, some women came to the tomb—and were they surprised!

The soldiers were gone, and the rock was rolled to the side.

389

The body of Jesus was not there!

But angels were there to tell the women the great news:

"JESUS IS ALIVE!"

And He is alive
today because
He really is God's Son.

397

He has risen, just as he said.
Matthew 28:6, NIV

1. What did the people who didn't like Jesus do to Him?

2. What was the good news the angels told the women?

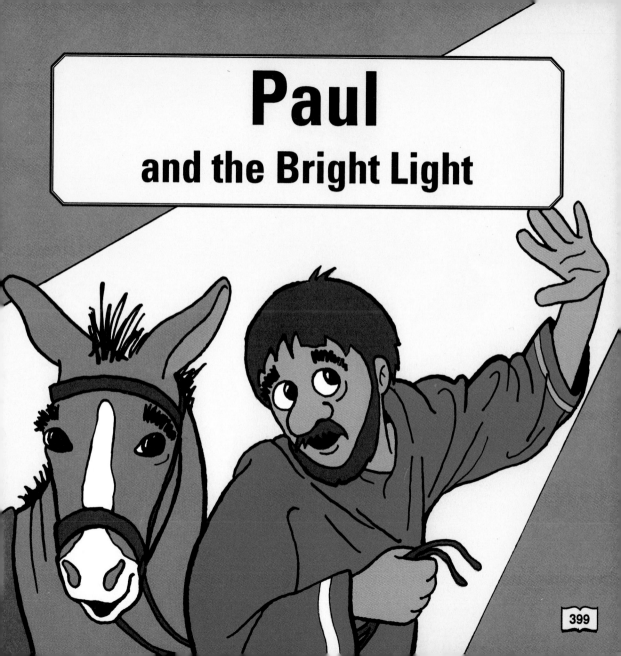

Paul
and the Bright Light

Paul was a Pharisee—
a religious teacher
of the Jews.

One day he heard a man named Stephen telling about Jesus.

The people listening to Stephen grew angry at what he said.

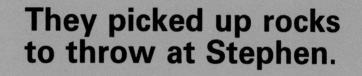

They picked up rocks
to throw at Stephen.

405

Since the Pharisees did not like Jesus, either, Paul was happy to help. He held the people's coats so they could throw better.

And he was glad when Stephen was dead.

408

Paul wanted to stop more people from telling about Jesus.

The other Pharisees told
Paul he could catch
followers of Jesus and
put them in jail.

410

Paul went to a city called
Damascus to find some
followers of Jesus.
But before he got there,
a bright light shone
on him from heaven.

As the light was shining,
Jesus spoke to Paul
from heaven.

Paul became a follower
of Jesus, too!

The bright light made Paul blind, so he had to be led into the city.

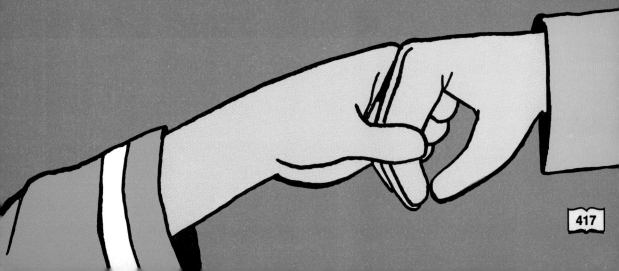

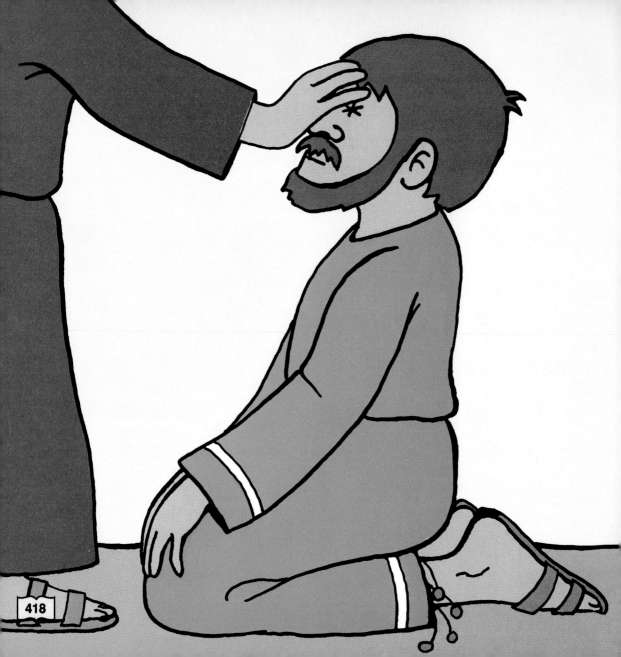

After three days, Ananias, another follower of Jesus, was sent by God to help Paul see again.

At first the followers of Jesus thought it was a trick by Paul to catch them—and you can't blame them!

But finally everyone believed him. Then the Pharisees tried to stop Paul from telling about Jesus!

**Even though Paul began
as an enemy of Jesus, God had
a job for him to do.**

Through Paul's work, news about Jesus was spread to the whole world.

Let your light shine.
Matthew 5:16, NIV

1. What did Paul do when he believed in Jesus?

2. Who did Paul tell about Jesus?